Jes the King

Story by Penny Frank
Illustrated by John Hayson

THE LION
STORY BIBLE

46

TRING · BELLEVILLE · SYDNEY

The Bible tells us how God sent his Son Jesus to show us what God is like, and to tell us how we can belong to God's kingdom.

This is the story of the last visit Jesus made to Jerusalem. You can find it in your own Bible in Matthew's Gospel, chapter 21.

Copyright © 1984 Lion Publishing

Published by
Lion Publishing plc
Icknield Way, Tring, Herts, England
ISBN 0 85648 771 6
Lion Publishing Corporation
10885 Textile Road, Belleville,
Michigan 48111, USA
ISBN 0 85648 771 6
Albatross Books
PO Box 320, Sutherland, NSW 2232, Australia
ISBN 0 86760 556 1

First edition 1984

Printed and bound in Hong Kong
by Mandarin Offset International (HK) Ltd.

British Library Cataloguing in Publication Data

Frank, Penny
    Jesus the King. – (The Lion Story
    Bible; 46)
    1. Jesus Christ – Entry into Jerusalem
    – Juvenile literature
    I. Title   II. Hayson, John
    232.9'5   BT415

    ISBN 0-85648-771-6

'Jesus is coming, Jesus is coming,'
the people said to each other in
Jerusalem.

The city was full of people, ready for
the Passover Festival.

Crowds of people rushed out to the
main road. They waited for a long time
and at last they saw him coming,
riding on a donkey.

The people pulled off their cloaks and
spread them down on the road for the
donkey to walk on.

Then they pulled branches down
from the trees and waved them as Jesus
rode by.

4

'Hurrah! God bless the king who comes in the name of the Lord!' they shouted. 'Praise God's name!'

The crowd was pleased to see Jesus come to Jerusalem. Many years ago the prophets had written that their king would ride into Jerusalem on a donkey. Now, here he was!

In Jerusalem Jesus went to God's temple with all the other people.

In the courtyard there was a market. There was a lot of noise.

When Jesus saw the money-changers cheating people he was really angry.

'God's temple is meant to be a house for prayer but you have made it like a hide-out for thieves. Get out!' Jesus shouted.

He ran through the market pushing over the tables and spilling all the money.

There were many blind beggars and lame people at the entrance to the temple. They came to Jesus and he made them well.

For the first time in their lives, the blind people could see the temple and the lame people could jump about.

The children cheered and shouted.

Many of the priests in the temple
had decided that Jesus was dangerous
because the people listened to him.
They were trying to find a way to kill
him.

'We have waited long enough,' they
all agreed. 'It's time to get rid of Jesus.'

But God had already told his Son what his plans were. Jesus knew he had to be in Jerusalem, even though the men were planning to kill him.

A few days later Jesus asked his
disciples to prepare the special Passover
meal so that they could eat together.
  Jesus was sad because he knew
it was the last time he would have
a meal with his disciples.

In the evening Jesus and his disciples met together in an upstairs room. Everything was ready for the meal.

The disciples' feet were dusty from the long day. Jesus took off his cloak and knelt down to wash their feet. He dried them with a towel.

The disciples said, 'This can't be right.
You are our master. You shouldn't be
doing the servant's work.'

'It is the servant's work,' said Jesus.
'I wanted to show you that my
followers must learn to serve each
other.'

15

They sat down to the special meal.
When they were eating Jesus said,
'One of you is going to help my
enemies catch me.'

They were so horrified by what Jesus had said that they did not notice Judas going out of the room. He was going to tell the priests how they could catch Jesus.

Then Jesus took some bread.

He said thank you to God, then he broke the bread up so that there was some on each plate.

'Eat this now,' he said. 'Soon my body will be broken for you just like this bread.'

Then Jesus took a cup of wine.

He said thank you to God, then he passed it round and they all drank from it.

'Drink this now,' he said. 'I am going to die and my blood will be poured out for you, like this wine.'

After the meal Jesus and the disciples went for a walk.

Jesus said, 'All of you are going to run away and leave me.'

The disciples were all upset and Simon Peter said, 'I don't care what anyone else does. I will never let you down.'

Jesus said, 'But you will, Simon Peter.
You'll even say that you don't know me.'
Simon Peter said, 'I'll never do that!'
And so did all the other disciples.

21

Then they went to one of the places they loved best–the garden of olive trees at Gethsemane.

Jesus went away on his own to pray, to talk to God his Father.

All the disciples felt sad. They did not understand. They were afraid.

A few days before, the people had shouted, 'God bless the king who comes in the name of the Lord.' Now Jesus was saying he had to die.

The disciples did not know that Jesus was a very special king of a very special kingdom.

What was going to happen next?

The Lion Story Bible is made up of 52 individual stories for young readers, building up an understanding of the Bible as one story – God's story – a story for all time and all people.

The New Testament section (numbers 31-52) covers the life and teaching of God's Son, Jesus. The stories are about the people he met, what he did and what he said. Almost all we know about the life of Jesus is recorded in the four Gospels – Matthew, Mark, Luke and John. The word gospel means 'good news'.

The last four stories in this section are about the first Christians, who started to tell others the 'good news', as Jesus had commanded them – a story which continues today all over the world.

The story of *Jesus the King* is told in all four Gospels: Matthew, chapter 21; Mark, chapter 11, Luke, chapter 19; John, chapter 12. Long before Jesus was born, God had promised to send his people a king to be their Saviour. He was to be a king of peace, so he would come riding a donkey, not a war-horse. The words of the Old Testament prophets came true the day that Jesus rode into Jerusalem. The people were wild with joy. No one but Jesus knew that just a few days later he would be facing death with no one to support him.

The next book in the series, number 47: *Jesus on trial*, continues the story.